Author: Jane Hammerslough
Illustrator: Andrea Morandi
Designers: Bill Henderson and Deena Fleming

Jane Hammerslough is the author of more than 20 books for young readers,
including *Owl Puke* and the *Dinosaurs Fandex Family Field Guide*.
She and her family split their time between Connecticut and California.

To Adam Rosenthal

an imprint of
■SCHOLASTIC
www.scholastic.com

Scholastic and Tangerine Press and associated logos are trademarks of
Scholastic Inc.

Published by Tangerine Press, an imprint of Scholastic Inc., 557 Broadway;
New York, NY 10012

10 9 8 7 6 5 4 3 2 1

ISBN (0-439-85278-1)

Printed and bound in China

CONTENTS

INTRODUCTION

Have you ever thought about what might be buried deep in the earth around you? How about everything from fossilized dinosaur dung that's millions of years old, to perfectly preserved woolly mammoths, ancient animal guts, and nature-made mummies!

If you're interested in some of the strangest stuff on Earth, you've come to the right place. Packed with cool facts, explanations of how natural artifacts manage to survive for millions of years, activities, and more, this book explores the lives of ancient animals, plants, and even humans through the remarkable—and often, downright disgusting—window of near-perfect preservation.

So sit back, relax, and get ready to explore the incredible world of prehistoric poop, mummified mammoths—and, believe it or not, ancient butter!— to name just a few of the weird remains that have lasted through time. And who knows—someday scientists and students might be studying something you, uh, produced!

FOUL

Dinosaurs lived *large*. Roaming the earth millions of years ago, many species were capable of devouring hundreds of pounds of prey or plants in a single feeding session. The end result of all those super-sized meals? You guessed right: Whether you call it poop, scat, feces, turds, or dung, dinosaurs produced huge quantities of it. In fact, scientists believe that members of the sauropod group of dinosaurs— long-necked plant eaters who were the biggest animals ever to live on land—may have produced over a *ton* of dung a day.

FOSSILS

Tracing Through Time

Body fossils are direct remains of ancient animals or plants, such as bones and teeth. Trace fossils are remains of past activity. They include footprints, tracks, burrows, eggs, nests, teeth marks, and fossilized waste, and give important clues about the behavior of ancient animals.

TURD TIMELINE

443-417 MYA
In the remains of the earliest known wildfire during the Silurian period, scientists discover one of the earliest known coprolites—a tiny millipede scat!

417-354 MYA
Fish, sharks, and the first amphibians are petrified poop-producers from the "age of fishes"—the Devonian period.

MYA = MILLIONS OF YEARS AGO

6

Most of the massive amount of solid waste that dinosaurs created disappeared through disintegration during the animals' lifetime, of course. But incredibly, some has survived to this day in fossilized form. People have discovered petrified poop—also known as **coprolite**—everywhere from England, where massive marine creatures once swam in now-dry sea beds, to areas of the Americas and Europe, where Tyrannosaurus rex and other meat eaters hunted; from ancient riverbeds in Asia to old tidal swamps in Africa, where herbivorous giants became prey for fierce meat eaters. Dating back more than 400 million years, coprolite provides a remarkable fossil record of some of the earliest creatures on Earth.

Dino poop—along with other coprolites from now-extinct mammals, reptiles, amphibians, and other animals—tell remarkable stories about what life was like for creatures who lived millions of years ago. Providing precise clues about what food ancient animals ate, what they may have looked like, where and when they lived, and what their relationships with other creatures in their environments were like, coprolites offer a rich portrait of prehistoric times.

A Rose by Any Other Name Would, uh, Smell . . .
In 1829, Anglican priest and geologist William Buckland coined the term coprolite from two Greek words, kopros, meaning "dung," and lithos, meaning "stone." The first to recognize fossilized dung and its importance in learning about ancient animals, Buckland was also the first person to name a dinosaur species, discovering and dubbing Megalosaurus in 1824.

354-290 MYA
During the Carboniferous period, the first reptiles and cockroaches appeared, depositing dung in the swamps that were forming and growing at this time.

290-248 MYA
Coprolite specimens from the Permian period—the "age of amphibians"—include those of marine animals that contain scales and bones.

And every one is distinct in its own way. Researchers have discovered coprolites—from dinosaurs and other prehistoric animals—which have included fossilized teeth, bone, fur, fish

Freeze-Dried Feces

Not all coprolites are created equal. Scientists have discovered dung dating back to the Pleistocene epoch—between 1.8 million and 10,000 years ago—that dried out, protected in caves or permafrost. Unlike older, fossilized specimens, "freeze-dried" scat can be analyzed biochemically, providing incredibly detailed clues into animals' pasts.

248-208 MYA
The Triassic period—when the first dinosaurs, crocodilians, and mammals appeared—features coprolites containing bones of the poop-producers' prey.

208-146 MYA
Large herbivores—sauropods—distributed seeds from the first flowering plants in their dung during the Jurassic period.

scales, shells, and a variety of plants, seeds, pollen, wood chips, fungus, insects, larvae, carved-out beetle burrows, and other items. Each unique specimen connects us to a living, breathing individual animal that lived thousands, if not millions, of years ago.

146-65 MYA
In the Cretaceous period, dinosaurs' heyday, dung discoveries come from a variety of marine and land animals—including the Tyrannosaurus rex!

PETRIFIED POOP PRODUCTION

While dinosaurs created breathtaking (gasp!) amounts of waste, only a small amount has lasted to this day. How does a piece of poop become a poop-shaped piece of rock over millions of years?

Fossilization begins when bone, shells, wood, plants, and other organic materials are buried in sediment, sand, ash, or mud that settles in the bottom of lakes, swamps, rivers, and other bodies of water. Sediments and water covering the remains protect them from the elements, bacteria, and other things that cause them to decay, decompose, and disappear. Over millions of years, as environ-

65-1.8 MYA
As dinosaurs die out, new mammals appear during the Tertiary period. Ancestors of modern-day animals—including humans—produce poop that gives important clues about the environment and adaptation.

1.8 million-11,000 years ago
Ice Age animals and humans are Earth's top poop producers, and their coprolites shed light on diet, lifestyle, and survival.

ments change, sediment layers continue to collect, eventually becoming hard rock.

In the meantime, what happens to that bone, shell, or dung? Water carrying dissolved minerals flows down into the earth, and those minerals seep into microscopic holes in the bone or other material. Sometimes, the minerals collect to form a hollow mold of the original material, which eventually decomposes. (Scientists make casts from these hollow molds to see what the ancient material looked like.) But sometimes, minerals actually replace all of the original material, preserving its original form. (Coprolites are created this way.) Either way, the result is a fossil, a precise mineral reproduction of something that existed in the distant past.

11,000 years ago-Present
Poop happens, and scientists use coprolites from this period to learn about the diets of early humans. And who knows? Today's discarded dung may be a paleontologist's prize specimen in the future!

COPROLITE HALL OF FAME: DINO POOP EXTREMES

Although dinosaurs produced massive amounts of poop, individual coprolites are often small—less than four inches (10 cm) long—compared with the sizes of the animals that produced them. (Think of current-day scat pellets, smaller than marbles, that deer and elk deposit.) But some prehistoric poop was huge. The largest coprolite ever unearthed was discovered in Saskatchewan, Canada. Believed to have been produced by a carnivore who lived 65 million years ago, the dino dung was a whopping 17 inches (43 cm) long, nearly seven inches (18 cm) wide, and made up of waste—more than half of it bones—that would have filled more than two and a half quart-sized containers! Usually, it is almost impossible to say exactly what kind of dinosaur produced a coprolite. But given this coprolite's great size, location, age, and bone content, scientists believe just one type of dinosaur could have created such an impressive specimen: none other than Tyrannosaurus rex!

REMARKABLE REMAINS: QUICK QUIZ

True or false? Like the California Gold Rush, between 1850 and 1890, Cambridgeshire, England, saw a "Coprolite Mining Rush" when thousands of people dug up petrified poop to sell.

(Answer: True. It was powdered and sold as fertilizer!)

Deadly Dino Farts?

Why did dinosaurs become extinct? According to some scientists, dino farts actually could have killed off the creatures! They believe that plant eaters released huge amounts of methane gas after eating all that vegetation—and it may have damaged the earth's ozone layer in prehistoric times, resulting in changing climates and food shortages. (And just imagine how it <u>smelled</u>....)

REMARKABLE REMAINS: QUICK QUIZ

The dinosaur species named for a university is called:

a. Harvardatops
b. Yaleosaurus
c. Stanfordopteryx
d. Princetonodon

(Answer: b)

DUNG SURVIVAL

It takes a special set of circumstances for poop to survive. Its content—from what the animal ate to how much water it contained—and its location, from where it was originally, uh, dropped, to how it was buried in sediment, all play a role in whether it eventually becomes a coprolite.

Here's the ideal situation for poop preservation:

1. After chowing down heartily on prey, a meat-eating dino takes a dump on a floodplain, or at the edge of a pond, swamp, stream, or other body of water. (The high calcium content of bones in meat eaters' poop makes it more likely to survive than poop containing plants, which breaks down more quickly.)
2. The poop dries slightly, retaining its shape.
3. A flash flood or other event quickly buries the poop in sediment underwater.
4. Fast forward millions of years, and presto! Petrified poop!

DINO DETECTIVE INVESTIGATION: ANATOMY OF A PREHISTORIC POOP PILE

When you hold a piece of petrified poop in your hand, speaking to it may not be the first thing you think of doing. But actually, if you know what to look for, that ancient turd can "talk" to you about the past. Here's what it might "say". . .

Bone chunks and other stuff with tooth marks show that the creature who produced this coprolite liked its meals meaty. These bones show that the dinosaur didn't chew or grind its food completely (some species of carnivores have teeth that do not meet together) but was able to break bones into fragments.

Even though dinosaurs had powerful digestive systems to process what they ate, they couldn't digest everything they ingested. The bones here show the animal's digestive tract was tough enough to handle sizeable bone pieces, eliminating what it couldn't digest.

The diameter of the bone chunks and traces of muscle tissue help show the size and type of prey the dinosaur ate. In this example, scientists might determine that the bones present came from an animal the size of a bear . . . so the creator of this specimen could have been a whole lot larger than that!

Tiny tracks and burrows in the coprolite show that other creatures made use of dino dung, digging through it for use as a home or for food, like modern dung beetles do.

A DAY IN THE LIFE OF DIPLODOCUS: DINNERTIME, ALL THE TIME

Diplodocus—tall as a four-story building—spent virtually all of its waking moments searching for food and chowing down. Because Diplodocus needed a huge amount of food each day, it may have sped up the digestive process by swallowing rocks along with evergreens, ferns, and other trees and plants.

Called gizzard stones, or **gastroliths,** these stones tumbled about in the stomach to help break down plant fibers and remained inside the animal for years.

In fact, both gastroliths and coprolites have actually been found *inside* dinosaur skeletons!

SCAT SIGHTINGS: FINDING COPROLITE

SASKATCHEWAN, CANADA

ENGLAND

MONTANA, USA

KANSAS, USA

NEW JERSEY, USA

NEW MEXICO, USA

REMARKABLE REMAINS: QUICK QUIZ

Paleontologists have discovered:

a. fossilized vomit

b. fossilized guts

c. fossilized blood vessels

d. all of the above

(Answer: d)

REMARKABLE REMAINS: QUICK QUIZ

True or false? Dinosaur coprolites are always found near dinosaur bones.

(Answer: False. Dinosaur coprolites have been found far from bones, showing that the animals may have traveled, relieving themselves while on the move.)

REMARKABLE REMAINS: QUICK QUIZ

True or false? The shape of a coprolite isn't important to scientists.

(Answer: False. A flattened shape might tell scientists something about the height of the animal that produced it—call it the "splat" factor—along with the dung's water content.)

CENTRAL INDIA

THAILAND

TREE

Say you're a young lizard living in a forest 50 million years ago. You're scampering along a tree trunk in search of something tasty, when suddenly, you're totally stuck. What's happening? Some weird, thick liquid you didn't notice before is holding you to the tree like Krazy Glue®. Even worse, there's more of that sticky stuff oozing out of the tree bark. And it's headed toward you . . . .

Flash ahead to present day, and that lizard is now perfectly preserved in an ultra-lightweight, transparent substance called amber. Formed from liquid tree resin—called "tree spit" by some—that has hard-ened over millions of years, amber contains ancient life forms, offering an extraordinary glimpse of plants and animals as they appeared millions of years ago. In vivid detail, amber's "frozen drama" often captures the behavior, interactions, and struggles of now-extinct life-forms who are the distant ancestors of those we see today.

SPIT

Amazing Amber: Fast Facts

- Amber has been found on every continent except Antarctica. Deposits on the shores of the Baltic Sea and in the Dominican Republic are the largest in the world.
- The oldest amber dates back about 225 million years.
- Amber can be transparent or cloudy, and usually ranges in color from nearly clear to shades of yellow, brown, and red. Rare blue and green amber result from minerals in surrounding sediments.
- The largest piece of transparent amber ever excavated weighed about 33 pounds (12 kg).
- More than 1,000 extinct species of insects have been identified in amber.

REMARKABLE REMAINS: QUICK QUIZ

For every human in the world, scientists estimate there are:

a. 200 million insects
b. 20 million insects
c. 20,000 insects
d. 2,000 insects

(Answer: a)

AMBER TIMELINE

345-225 MYA
During the Paleozoic era, resin-producing plants began to appear, producing the earliest amber. Very rare, tiny amber pieces containing a variety of early plant specimens have been found in Scottish coal mines.

MYA = MILLIONS OF YEARS AGO

225-65 MYA
The Mesozoic era—which includes the Triassic, Jurassic, and Cretaceous periods, when dinosaurs roamed—resulted in amber, now brittle and scarce due to its age. Amber specimens from this time have been found all over the world, and include insects as well as ancient plants, including the oldest-known mushroom and flowers, both about 90 million years old.

65-54 MYA
Amber specimens from start of the Cenozoic era—which includes present time—include plants, insects, and other creatures. Most specimens from this time period are from ancient lagoons and riverbeds in Russia and England.

54-24 MYA
During this time, amber continued to form in the Baltic region and in areas of Europe, Asia, Africa, North America, and South America. Some of this period's largest and most interesting amber specimens include ants, wasps, frogs, and lizards, among other animals from the Dominican Republic.

Resin is the sticky substance that trees produce. It is distinct from sap, the waterlike fluid, sometimes containing sugars, that circulates throughout trees. (Maple syrup is created by boiling and condensing the sap from maple trees.) While all trees produce sap, only certain trees create resin. When resin petrifies, it becomes amber.

Amber specimens are different from other natural artifacts because they are not true fossils. When a living thing or other organic matter becomes a fossil, each original cell is replaced by minerals. But in amber, the original cells of an organism still exist after millions of years. What you see inside amber are the actual animal or plant remains.

24-5 MYA
Over time, resin-producing plants sprung up in other areas. Amber from this time period has been found in New Zealand, Romania, Borneo, and many other diverse places. Butterflies, spiders, bird feathers, and fur inclusions date from this time.

5 MYA-Present
Most amber is more than five million years old, but people's interest in amber dates back to prehistoric times. Today, it is still prized as a gem and as an amazing scientific record of the past.

Things that are stuck in amber are called **inclusions.** And what inclusions there are! Seeds, bark, buds, leaves, and other remnants of ancient plant life show small pieces of the world in which great reptiles and giant mammals once lived. And amber inclusions show us the smaller animals who shared that world, from a prehistoric fly caught in the middle of laying eggs to a frog that may have been another animal's discarded dinner, from cockroaches, termites, and stingless bees to tufts of early mammal hair and feathers from some of the first birds on Earth. Like no other fossil record, amber opens a window into the past that allows us to see true prehistoric life, frozen in time.

REMARKABLE REMAINS: QUICK QUIZ

True or false? In 1492, when Christopher Columbus arrived at the island of Hispaniola (now the Dominican Republic and Haiti), he gave a Taino chief European amber beads—and coincidentally, received a pair of shoes decorated with Caribbean amber in return.

(Answer: True. The largest deposits of amber are found in Eastern Europe and the Dominican Republic; it was prized in both places.)

WHY RESIN ROCKS

Resin, which oozes and drips through bark, protects trees from disease and fungi, and helps heal wounds such as broken branches. Its strong aroma may repel insects who cause damage or attract those who help with pollination. The next time you see an evergreen, look for shiny, liquid resin on the trunk. Smell it—some say the scent of resin from different kinds of trees reminds them of vanilla, butterscotch, or pine. Touch it and you'll immediately know why all sorts of things could get stuck in it!

Which, of course, they did, millions of years ago. Once a drop of resin trapped a creature, it was stuck there. The sticky resin kept flowing, and as "nature's flypaper," layers slowly built up and began to harden, encasing insects and other creatures, seeds and other plant parts, and natural artifacts, such as animal hair, in an airtight case.

Amber Lore

Called "gold of the north" and
"petrified sunlight," amber has always
fascinated people. Featured in ancient myths
from all over the world, amber has been treasured as a gem, traded,
and carved into art forms for more than 10,000 years.
Why? A natural plastic, amber is different from minerals and
gems. Unlike cold, heavy stones, it is warm to the touch and so
lightweight it floats in salt water. When it's rubbed, amber releases
a light scent and becomes charged with static electricity, attracting
small particles like a magnet. (The Greek name for amber is
elektron, or "sun-made.")

In the past, people believed amber could enhance the powers of
magicians and sorcerers, protect people against evil, and offer
cures for many illnesses, including the black plague, asthma, and
gout. Nicias, an ancient Athenian, described amber as "juice of the
setting sun, congealed in the sea and cast up on the shore." Today,
it is still prized by collectors for its unique beauty and connection
to the past.

A MERE SHELL OF HIS OR HER FORMER SELF

Most animals found in amber were exposed to some oxygen, so their internal organs have been lost to time. However, some whole animals were completely sealed by resin—and their inner parts are still intact!

But it took more than just oozing down a tree trunk to create the right environment for amber to form. When exposed to oxygen in the air, resin breaks down. So for the resin to become amber, it soon had to be covered by dense sediments—clay or sand in a lagoon or riverbed— that kept out oxygen.

TERRIFIC TERPENES

Why are animals found in amber so amazingly well preserved? Scientists believe that terpenes are the answer. Terpenes, strong-smelling chemicals in resin, kill bacteria that normally would cause a creature to decay. Additionally, terpenes in resin may cause tissue to dehydrate, or dry out, without shrinking. If you've ever found, say, a dead, dried-up spider, you know that's pretty unusual!

Over many years, resin terpenes change the substance from a sticky liquid to a lightweight solid. That process is called **polymerization**. The extraordinary properties of resin terpenes, combined with burial and time, result in long-extinct creatures, suspended in golden, natural plastic, that look nearly alive.

DINO CLONES? THE GREAT DNA DEBATE

How cool would it be to clone a T. rex, Compsognathus, or another "terrible reptile" from the past? In the movie *Jurassic Park*, scientists do just that, using dinosaur DNA from mosquitoes who'd bitten the beasts—then got stuck in amber! Could it ever really happen?

Even though amber is great at preserving things, DNA— the "building blocks" of life-forms—breaks down over time. Finding complete DNA in amber millions of years old is impossible, say scientists. And there are other challenges, such as putting that DNA in the right order to get an animal's genetic code. That's kind of like piecing together a billion-piece jigsaw puzzle—without a guide!

So let's just say you did have complete, orderly DNA. Next, you would have to assemble the animal's chromosomes and find a living egg that would accept the whole thing so it could grow—which is about as likely as, well, finding a velociraptor in your backyard.

So, even though amber is awesome, it probably won't be bringing back dinosaurs anytime soon. But it's an amazing idea, isn't it?

INCREDIBLE INCLUSIONS

So what, exactly, got trapped by the resin that eventually became amber? And why?

When it comes to being preserved in amber, size matters. The most common inclusions are insects—which, dating back about 350 million years, are some of the oldest creatures on Earth—that were blown by the wind or simply stepped into resin. Larger animals usually had enough strength to escape the sticky stuff, though some rare amber specimens show the bones and other remains of much bigger creatures, discarded after being eaten by another animal.

Some amber inclusions show animal behavior and relationships between creatures—and between plants and animals—in the past. Others ended up together for eternity by accident, simply getting stuck in the same, sticky flow of resin. Either way, when creatures were in precisely the wrong place at the wrong time, it resulted in a wealth of information about extinct animal species and their environments.

TAKE A BIG BREATH

Amber traps more than little plants and creatures: Scientists from the U.S. Geological Survey recently tested air bubbles in amber to determine changes in the earth's atmosphere. Their findings? Sixty-seven million years ago, air contained about 35 percent more oxygen than it does today! Were higher oxygen levels essential for dinosaurs' survival? The answer is still up for debate, but one thing is clear. The drop in oxygen levels happened gradually over millions of years, at the same time dinosaurs became extinct!

AMBER SPECIMENS HAVE INCLUDED:

- ☑ a group of ants and a large millipede, which scientists believe was going to be their dinner. Millions of years old, the specimen told scientists that ants had been social animals—who worked together for the good of their group—far longer into the past than they had supposed.

- ☑ mating pairs of insects and other creatures

- ☑ Earth's oldest mosquito, with mouth parts strong enough to pierce dinosaur skin (a)

- ☑ spiders capturing prey, with and without webs (b)

- ☑ bees, showing scientists that flowers existed in the same time, because bees needed the pollen from flowering plants

- ☑ an ancient termite worker feeding a termite soldier

- ☑ large animal teeth

- ☑ tiny mites clinging to larger insects as parasites

- ☑ perfectly preserved leaves, fruits, and flowers of extinct plants (c)

- ☑ a footprint, believed to be that of a prehistoric cat! (d)

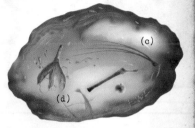

AMBER WAVES OF NEW JERSEY

While digging in abandoned
clay pits in Sayreville,
New Jersey, in the 1990s,
a local fossil collector
made a remarkable
discovery: the oldest
amber with inclusions
ever discovered in the
New World! To date, the
mine has yielded over
500 pounds (189 kg) of
amber that is more than 90
million years old. Experts
from the American Museum of
Natural History in New York City
have discovered more than 100 new
(well, very old) insect species
in this treasure trove.

SAYREVILLE, NEW JERSEY

REMARKABLE REMAINS: QUICK QUIZ

In ancient Rome:

a. amber was said to cost more than an enslaved human.

b. soldiers wore amber for good luck, and women dyed their hair to match amber.

c. Emperor Nero sent an expedition north in search of amber, establishing the "Amber Route."

d. all of the above

(Answer: d)

DID YOU KNOW?

Frankincense and myrrh are incense made from copal—hardened resin that is younger than amber—which still retains its smell through the presence of terpenes.

REMARKABLE REMAINS: QUICK QUIZ

True or false? All amber was produced from resin of trees that produce cones, such as pines.

(Answer: False. Although Baltic amber originated from pine trees, amber from the Dominican Republic was produced from the resin of a now-extinct species of broad-leaved tropical trees.

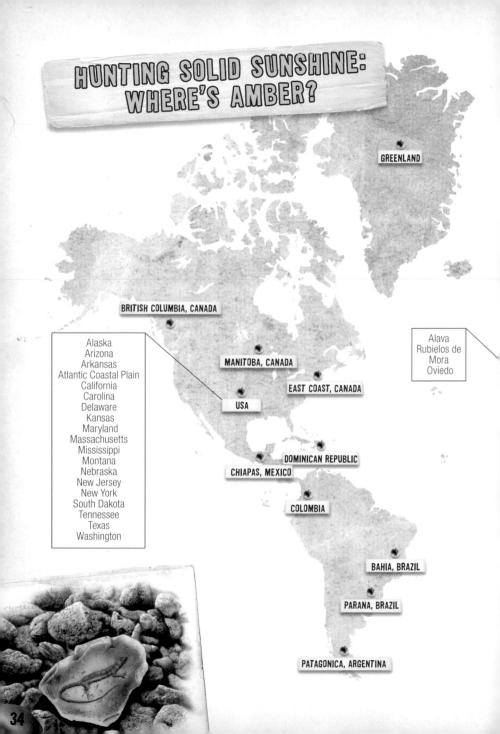

HUNTING SOLID SUNSHINE: WHERE'S AMBER?

GREENLAND

BRITISH COLUMBIA, CANADA

Alaska
Arizona
Arkansas
Atlantic Coastal Plain
California
Carolina
Delaware
Kansas
Maryland
Massachusetts
Mississippi
Montana
Nebraska
New Jersey
New York
South Dakota
Tennessee
Texas
Washington

Alava
Rubielos de Mora
Oviedo

MANITOBA, CANADA

EAST COAST, CANADA

USA

DOMINICAN REPUBLIC

CHIAPAS, MEXICO

COLOMBIA

BAHIA, BRAZIL

PARANA, BRAZIL

PATAGONICA, ARGENTINA

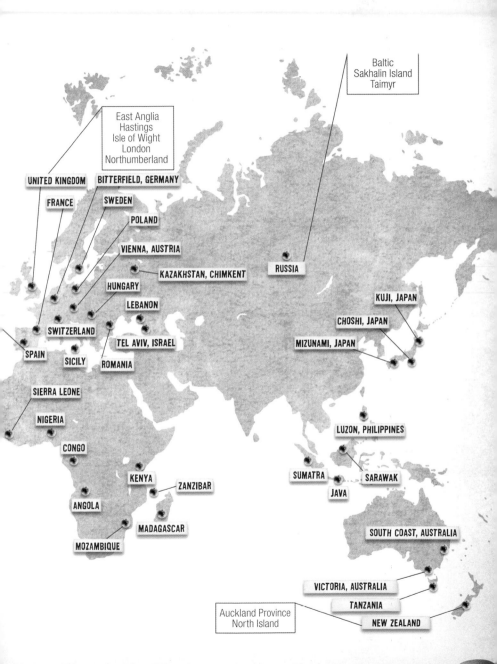

Baltic
Sakhalin Island
Taimyr

East Anglia
Hastings
Isle of Wight
London
Northumberland

UNITED KINGDOM
BITTERFIELD, GERMANY
FRANCE
SWEDEN
POLAND
VIENNA, AUSTRIA
KAZAKHSTAN, CHIMKENT
RUSSIA
HUNGARY
LEBANON
KUJI, JAPAN
CHOSHI, JAPAN
SWITZERLAND
MIZUNAMI, JAPAN
TEL AVIV, ISRAEL
SPAIN
SICILY
ROMANIA
SIERRA LEONE
NIGERIA
LUZON, PHILIPPINES
CONGO
KENYA
ZANZIBAR
SUMATRA
SARAWAK
JAVA
ANGOLA
MADAGASCAR
MOZAMBIQUE
SOUTH COAST, AUSTRALIA
VICTORIA, AUSTRALIA
TANZANIA
Auckland Province
North Island
NEW ZEALAND

FROZEN

F or the family out herding reindeer on the Siberian steppe, it was strange enough to stumble upon a huge, curved pair of tusks sticking up out of the ice. But they were even more stunned to find that those tusks were attached to an enormous head of a hairy creature that had been extinct for a good ten thousand years!

The ancient animal, a woolly mammoth nicknamed Zharkov in honor of the family who discovered him, had died about 23,000 years ago. And yet, complete with tusks, fur, and flesh, the animal's entire body remained encased in a 20-ton chunk of ice and dirt. A male that stood about nine feet (2.7 m) tall and is believed to have been 47 years old when it died, deep-frozen Zharkov is the best-preserved, most intact adult mammoth specimen ever discovered.

IN TIME

Exposure to warmer or more humid conditions than the deep freeze where the animal had been residing for thousands of years would cause it to begin decaying very quickly. To continue preserving and studying the animal, scientists airlifted Zharkov by helicopter to a frigid, dry cave dug in the permafrost inside the Arctic Circle. Working in that cold, outdoor lab, they carefully dissected the creature. Today, scientists continue to seek out clues to the past by studying Zharkov and the remains of other Ice Age mammals.

THE LEGEND OF THE GIANT RODENT

For thousands of years, ivory traders have sought out huge tusks and bones on the Siberian steppe. Ancient legend said these natural artifacts came from giant rodents, who lived in a remote underworld. The old story claimed that these huge, hairy rodents died when exposed to light and brought bad luck to anyone who saw them! It was only in the early 1800s, when botanist Mikhail Adams investigated stories of a huge carcass imbedded in ice that the myth was challenged and the first frozen mammoth was unearthed and identified! Today, the 37,000-year-old skeleton, whose bones alone weigh more than a ton, is on display at the Russian Academy of Sciences Museum in St. Petersburg.

WOOLLY MAMMOTH TIMELINE

4 MYA
Mammoths appear in southern and eastern Africa. They migrate north, moving across Europe and Eurasia to Siberia.

1.7 MYA
Mammoths cross the land bridge that linked Siberia and Alaska.

MYA = MILLIONS OF YEARS AGO

Meet Baby Dima!

In 1977, a gold miner working in northeastern Siberia found an unusual treasure: a beautifully preserved, 40,000-year-old male baby woolly mammoth. Just three and a half feet (1 m) tall with a trunk that about 23 inches (58 cm) long, the ancient pachyderm, later dubbed "Dima," was too young to have tusks. Believed to have died at the age of six months, Dima closely resembled a modern elephant with fur, but his ears were tiny—just one tenth the size of a modern African elephant baby!

700,000-500,000 years ago
Adapting to colder climates, steppe mammoths develop, distinct from ancestral mammoths who remained in warmer climates.

350,000 years ago
Woolly mammoths appear. Long fur, different teeth, and other adaptations enable them to survive cooler climates and a change in diet.

Magnificent Mammoths: Fast Facts

- Most mammoths lived between about four million and 10,000 years ago, after dinosaurs became extinct. They lived all over the world, ranging in height from about six feet (1.8 m) tall to more than 15 feet (5 m) tall.
- Woolly mammoths weighed about 200 pounds (76 kg) at birth, and could weigh more than 15,000 pounds (5,600 kg) as adults. They usually lived about 60 years, traveling in herds headed by females.
- Some mammoth species had straight tusks; others were deeply curved, reaching lengths of more than 17 feet (5 m). The animals used their tusks to fight, communicate in mating, and dig for food.
- Woolly mammoths had thick, long hair—up to three feet (.9 m) long! Scientists have found that the animals molted, or shed, in the summer. A thick undercoat kept the animals warm in winter. Woolly mammoths also had a hairy, knoblike bump on their heads, and a high hump on their backs.

Unlike fossils, frozen specimens are preserved animals who actually lived many thousands of years ago. Though all the woolly mammoths found to date show some signs of "aging" either through decay, scavenging of other animals, or simply the passage of time, they provide an extraordinary opportunity to learn about lives (and sometimes, deaths) during the Ice Age.

350,000-15,000 years ago
Woolly mammoths live throughout permafrost regions in North America, Russia, and Europe.

15,000-12,000 years ago
The earth's climate changes and northern ice sheets begin to melt.

INCREDIBLE ICE

How does a mammoth ice cube get made? Why does it happen? The answer is in a preservation process that is as old as the earth and as close as your own kitchen. It begins, of course, with water.

Now, you probably know that water can take three different forms: gas (such as fog or steam), liquid (like the stuff you drink), and solid (ice). When the temperature of water drops below 32°F (0°C), it freezes, changing from a liquid to a solid. If the temperature stays below 32°F, water stays frozen.

DID YOU KNOW?

The word mammoth comes from *mamut*, an old Russian name for the big, hairy extinct beast and has come to mean anything enormous.

12,000-10,000 years ago
Mammoths become extinct in Europe and Asia.

10,000 years ago
Woolly mammoths die out in Siberia and the Americas.

Bon Appetit, Pleistocene Style!

R. Dale Guthrie, professor emeritus at the University of Alaska, didn't just excavate "Blue Babe," a 36,000-year-old frozen steppe bison. He also tried tasting it!

According to the U.S. Department of Agriculture, deep-frozen meat lasts indefinitely, an idea which Guthrie put to the test. With his colleagues, he defrosted, cleaned, and diced meat from the ancient animal's neck, added some stock, and simmered it with vegetables for a unique stew. "We had Blue Babe for dinner. The meat was well aged but still a little tough, and it gave the stew a strong Pleistocene aroma, but nobody there would have dared miss it," Guthrie wrote later.

DID YOU KNOW?

Scientists used hair dryers to defrost Zharkov's ice block inch by inch to carefully study and document the animal!

3,700 years ago
Dwarf mammoths living on Wrangell Island off the coast of Siberia become extinct.

Why was Professor Guthrie able to eat meat that was 36,000 years old and not get sick? When something is frozen, bacteria, molds, and yeasts become inactive. They simply stop growing or changing. If something isn't spoiled when it's frozen, such as a piece of pizza that was thrown into the freezer a couple of months ago, it won't be spoiled when you take it out, even months later. Chances are that if you defrost it and heat it up, it will still be edible. (Okay, maybe it won't taste great, but it will be edible!)

Some chemical processes are just slowed down—not stopped—by freezing, and over time, material may deteriorate somewhat. When frozen, the water in cells may expand and burst the cell. But all told, deep freezing is still a remarkable way of preserving things, even for 10,000 years or more!

REMARKABLE REMAINS: QUICK QUIZ

The mammoth species named for a U.S. president is called:

a. Jefferson's mammoth
b. Nixon's mammoth
c. Madison's mammoth
d. Kennedy's mammoth

(Answer: a. Thomas Jefferson was a great collector of Ice Age fossils!)

DID YOU KNOW?

Western Camels once roamed the Yukon! Camels living during the Ice Age resembled modern-day dromedaries but were about seven feet (2 m) tall. The animals' long legs and necks enabled them to reach high vegetation.

DID YOU KNOW?

American lions, Ice Age lions that lived in the Americas and Eurasia, were huge—about 25 percent bigger than African lions living today. These fast, agile predators competed with saber-toothed cats, wolves, and short-faced bears to feed on steppe bison, mammoths, and other prehistoric mammals.

SPOTLIGHT ON GEOLOGY: PERMAFROST

An ice age is a period of geologic time when the earth cools and ice covers a significant amount of the earth's surface. Scientists believe that there have been seven major ice ages. The last ice age peaked about 20,000 years ago; afterward, the earth began to warm up. Permafrost, a permanently frozen layer of soil under an "active" layer of soil that thaws during the summer, forms during an ice age. Today, about 20 percent of the earth is permafrost, which may be nearly a mile (1.6 km) deep in parts of Siberia.

How did woolly mammoths come to be preserved in the ice? After an animal died, perhaps as prey to large cats or humans, by a fall into a silt-filled pond or through the ice and starving to death, or by natural causes, its body temperature would begin to fall. If conditions were cold enough, it would freeze before decomposing. Over time, covered by dirt, ice, and snow, the deep-frozen creature would desiccate, or dry out, and remain preserved indefinitely.

THE WORLD'S SMELLIEST TUNNEL

Fairbanks, Alaska, is home to what may be the worst-smelling tunnel in history—or shall we say, prehistory. Dug through 40,000-year-old permafrost by the U.S. Army Corps of Engineers in the 1960s to test ways of tunneling in frozen environments, the tunnel is a true "cross section" of life from the past: Bones of extinct creatures and plants poke through the walls! For visitors viewing the jaw of a 14,000-year-old steppe bison, tiny snail shells, an ancient pond now permanently frozen, and other natural artifacts, a stroll through the tunnel is like taking a walk through time. But be warned: Because the creatures and plants are exposed to air and have begun to decay, the tunnel smells, well, awful. You might even say, like death!

CARCASS CLUES

To date, countless tusks and about fifty full or partial woolly mammoth carcasses have been found, revealing remarkable clues about how the animals lived and what their environment was like. The stomach contents of these creatures, for example, include large quantities of the now-extinct grasses and other plants the animals ate—about 400 pounds (151 kg) a day!

Changes in the tusk's rings and wear patterns reveal the creature's activity and health over the years, and may say something about the climate and food availability for each year of its life.

Tusks tell a story, too. Like trees, mammoth tusks grew in annual rings. (Each year, the tusks would get thicker.) A cross-section of a tusk reveals how old an animal was at the time of its death.

THE DNA DEBATE....AGAIN!

Could you create a twenty-first century woolly mammoth by cloning a frozen specimen? Despite the fact that scientists have extracted some intact DNA from these extinct animals, the answer is still no. (Sorry, sci-fi fans!) As time passes, cells deteriorate and cannot stand up to the complex process of cloning.

Its teeth might show signs of wear, which scientists believe came from the animal's chomping through ice to get water or chewing tough vegetation.

And of course, frozen woolly mammoth carcasses offer an up-close view of the internal organs of prehistoric animals like no other. By studying the inner workings of the animal—from muscles, cardio-vascular and pulmonary systems to blood, ancient viruses and even DNA—scientists may learn how woolly mammoths survived on the tundra...and perhaps, ultimately, why they perished.

The long, thick hair of a woolly mammoth carcass may carry pollen, seeds, and other traces of prehistoric plants.

SOME AWESOME ICE AGE MAMMALS

What other creatures lived alongside woolly mammoths? Check these out!

SLOTH: These giant creatures are ancestors of the modern tree sloth. They were plant eaters who probably ate the leaves found on the lower branches of trees. The largest of the ground sloths was Megatherium, which could grow to 20 feet (6 m) tall and weighed several tons. Fossils of the giant ground sloth were found in North and South America. One species of a giant ground sloth is the *Megalonyx jeffersonii*, named after Thomas Jefferson, one of the Founding Fathers of America. Jefferson was a paleontologist and first named the giant sloth Megalonyx, or "great claw," based on a fossil found in a West Virginia cave.

STEPPE BISON: Weighing upward of 1,800 pounds (681 kg), steppe bison were larger than modern buffaloes and had much longer horns. These giant plant eaters grazed on the Alaskan tundra during the Ice Age; cave paintings show that they were hunted by humans.

YUKON HORSES: Horses living alongside woolly mammoths were small—just four feet (1.2 m) tall at the withers, or tallest part of their backs. With broad heads and furry bodies, they resembled modern ponies.

PLEISTOCENE WOLVES: Smaller

than their modern counterparts,
these swift, prehistoric predators
traveled in packs, just as wolves do
today. Unlike most animals of the Ice
Age, wolves have survived, relatively
unchanged, in the Yukon region to
this day.

THE REAL GIANT RODENT

Some of the largest rodents
of all time, prehistoric
beavers were about eight feet
(2.4 m) long and weighed
upwards of 500 pounds (189
kg)! With ridged, six-inch
(15-cm) cutting teeth, these
giants built large lodges.

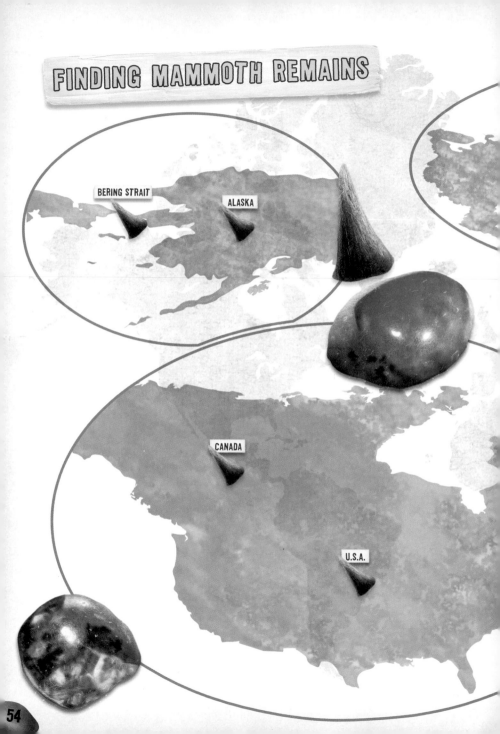

FINDING MAMMOTH REMAINS

BERING STRAIT

ALASKA

CANADA

U.S.A.

SIBERIA

BOGGED DOWN . . .

What do deer with antlers 14 feet (4.2 m) wide, huge logs of really old butter, and ancient humans have in common? They have all been found, often amazingly intact, in peat bogs around the world!

Bogs are special habitats found throughout Europe and North America. Though they often look like dry, solid ground covered with moss, don't be fooled: That moss is actually floating on a deep, decaying stew of more moss, plants, and water, called peat. Forget solid ground—if you step on a spongy bog, you might just sink! In fact, the word bog comes from an old Irish word meaning soft.

FOREVER

Boggy Beginnings

Imagine a bowl filled with dead plants and water. Okay, now imagine adding more water and dead plants. The water covering the plants would block oxygen, so they would not rot completely. Instead, the slow-decaying plants would begin to build up, forming layers of a substance called peat.

Bogs began to form about 10,000 years ago, at the end of the last ice age. As the years went by, sphagnum moss began to grow on the bogs, eventually dying off and becoming peat moss, which is harvested and used as a nutrient-rich fertilizer in garden soil.

BOG TIMELINE

10,000 years ago
Melting glaciers leave behind many small craters in land throughout Europe and other areas.

10,000-9,000 years ago
Lakes form in these craters. With poor drainage, moss begins to grow in these lakes.

MYA = MILLIONS OF YEARS AGO

When an animal or object ends up in a bog, how does the environment preserve it? The bog environment doesn't change much over time, so whatever ends up in a bog can remain undisturbed for thousands of years. Because the mixture of water and peat blocks oxygen, decay slows way down. (Oxygen is essential for decomposition.) To further preserve material, acid in sphagnum moss stops bacteria from growing, which enables the skin, hair, bones, and even internal organs to remain as they were in life, thousands of years later!

9,000-3500 years ago
Moss continues to grow, die, and remain in the water of the bog. Layers of dead moss build to form peat. The "lake" is no longer a body of water, but a peat bog.

3,500 years ago-Present
So much peat builds up in bogs that they become "raised" hills of peat covered with live moss. Prehistoric people use peat bogs for fuel, to mine iron, to store food, and for rituals, including human sacrifice!

The acid in sphagnum moss, called **spagnan**, works to "tan" things that remain in bogs for long periods of time. Just as an animal hide becomes leather through a process of tanning, spagnan preserves and turns the skin of animals, along with plants and other materials, a deep brown. Undisturbed for millennia beneath layers of peat that form an airtight time-cocoon, things may retain their shapes, down to the smallest details, until they are unearthed.

BOGGY MEN AND WOMEN

It's not only animals that are preserved in peat bogs. Hundreds and hundreds of humans who lived more than 2000 years ago have been found in European bogs. These eerie "bog mummies"—many still dressed in the clothes they wore thousands of years ago—are so lifelike they appear to be sleeping.

One of the most famous bog mummies is the "Tollund Man," discovered by a pair of brothers out cutting peat in a Danish bog in 1950. Wearing nothing more than a sheepskin cap, a belt, and a leather rope around his neck, the man was so well preserved that the brothers believed he was a recent murder victim and called the police! Carbon-14 dating revealed that the man had lived around 350 B.C., during the Iron Age.

Who was the Tollund Man? He was a small, slight man, just five feet three inches (1.5 m, 7.6 cm) tall, and about 40 years old when he

died. He had short hair under his pointed cap and visible stubble on his face. Scientists believe he did not shave the day of his death. Buried in the bog with his eyes and mouth closed, he remains in a curled position that looks like he is peacefully sleeping. During the time that the Tollund Man lived, most people were cremated. But scientists believe that care was taken with his burial, because he may have been a human sacrifice, perhaps to bog gods!

The Tollund Man's stomach revealed that his last meal was a gruel or soup made from thirty different kinds of plant seeds, including barley. A deep scar on his foot showed that he walked barefoot and injured himself, though his feet show signs of having worn shoes as well. With scars, wrinkles, hairs, and even fingerprints clearly visible, the Tollund Man is an amazing example of the power of preservation as a way of understanding the past.

FOR PEAT'S SAKE!

Peat bogs have been important to people for a long time. For thousands of years, dried peat has been used as fuel to heat houses. Sphagnum moss, which grows on top of bogs, is an antibacterial material that was dried and used for bandages during World War I. Even yucky, brown bog water, which probably isn't the tastiest beverage, was prized for long journeys, because it stayed algae-free longer than spring or well water!

NATURE-MADE MUMMIES

More than 1,500 human mummies have been found in bogs in Ireland, Scotland, England, the Netherlands, Germany, Denmark, and Sweden, often with flesh, bones, and even internal organs perfectly preserved. Other nature-made mummies have turned up over the years throughout the world. Here are a few kinds:

Sand Mummies

Long before King Tut, Egyptians simply buried bodies in hot sand, which dried them out, preserving both internal organs and skin! These natural mummies gave Egyptians the idea of helping the process along with chemicals, wrapping, and elaborate tombs—and the rest is, uh, history.

Ice Mummies

"Otzi the Ice Man," the oldest-known human mummy, was discovered in the Italian Alps. Thought to have been frozen while hunting 5,300 years ago, the tattooed, icy mummy was dressed for work and carried an ax, a knife, bow and arrows, a medicine bag, birch bark containers, and a backpack!

Freeze-dried Mummies

From the mountains of Peru and China to caves in the U.S., scientists have uncovered bodies preserved by cold, dry conditions. The Spirit Cave man, a mummy found wrapped in a rabbit fur robe in a cave in Churchill County, Nevada, is more than 10,000 years old, the oldest North American mummy ever found.

TRAPPED IN ASPHALT

While spongy peat bogs were preserving all manner of Ice Age plants and animals in northern Europe, another sort of natural trap was capturing their cohorts in what is now downtown Los Angeles! At the Rancho La Brea tar pits, natural asphalt deposits trapped hundreds of animals. Thanks to asphalt's airtight seal and chemical makeup, bones of these extinct creatures have been preserved perfectly. Since the early 1900s, when scientists began to explore the pits, more than three million specimens from about 650 species have been uncovered there, and excavations continue to this day.

If you've ever walked on a freshly paved road on a hot summer day, you know it can be a sticky situation, to say the least. It looks like solid ground until you begin to sink! Prehistoric pools of soft, oozy asphalt were often hidden by a thin layer of dirt or leaves. For the animals who wandered onto the pits, the situation wasn't just sticky, it was deadly.

NOT EXACTLY TAR PITS

It looks like a giant animal underneath the surface is burping. That's how some people describe the thick substance that bubbles up in the active pits at Rancho La Brea. La Brea means "tar" in Spanish, and most people refer to the area as tar pits, but actually, that sticky substance is asphalt. While tar is produced by burning peat or coal, asphalt occurs naturally.

REMARKABLE REMAINS: QUICK QUIZ

Geologists have discovered tar pits in:

a. Peru

b. Iran

c. other parts of California

d. all of the above

(Answer: d)

DID YOU KNOW?

Some bogs are 98 percent water and 2 percent peat, which can take more than fifty days to dry!

How does an asphalt pit form? Millions of years ago, the land that is now Los Angeles was under the Pacific Ocean. As marine animals died and were covered by sediments, they produced crude oil, a "fossil fuel." About 100,000 years ago, the ocean level went down, and the areas that had once been underwater became land. New layers of gravel, sand, and other material settled on top of the land.

But the oil from marine animals was still there. About 40,000 years ago, it began oozing through cracks in the layers of earth, eventually forming pools, or seep, on the earth's surface. As some of the oil slowly evaporated from the substance, it became thicker. Animals who wandered into natural asphalt pools would soon find themselves stuck—and easy prey for other animals. The packs of meat eaters who followed prey into the asphalt seep with hopes of an easy meal were in for an ugly surprise—the gooey substance trapped them, too!

REMARKABLE REMAINS: QUICK QUIZ

True or false? The bones of carnivores found in asphalt pits outnumber those of plant eaters ten to one.

(Answer: True. In search of a meaty meal, many more carnivorous predators and scavengers perished in the pits than herbivores, who simply got stuck by accident!)

Bacteria helped the fur, flesh, feathers, and other soft parts of animals stuck in the pits to decompose. The creatures' bones, however, became soaked with oily asphalt, which helped preserve them. Over thousands of years, more asphalt seeped in, and other sediments settled over the bones. As time passed, asphalt continued to ooze from below, sediments piled above, and cone-shaped hills emerged at the pools' sites.

BOG BUTTER

For years, peat cutters in Ireland and Scotland have been digging up large quantities of a very strange substance, stored in big barrels, baskets, or animal skins, which looked like 3,000-year-old butter. Recently, scientists have found that some of the specimens are indeed butter and other dairy products! They believe that people who lived during the Bronze Age stored food in bogs—sort of like an ancient refrigerator, minus the freezer—where it would stay cool and free of bacteria.

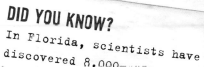

LURKING BELOW THE SURFACE

At Rancho La Brea, a virtual ecosystem has been preserved in fossilized form. Prehistoric plants, bugs, amphibians, reptiles, fish, birds, and mammals were all trapped in asphalt, providing an extraordinary glimpse of life between 40,000 and 10,000 years ago. Some extraordinary finds there include...

GROUND SLOTHS, ancestors of the modern-day animals who spend more than 20 hours a day sleeping in trees. At six feet (1.8 m) tall and 3,500 pounds (1,300 kg), prehistoric ground sloths lived on the ground, no doubt spending a fair amount of time searching for food!

SABER-TOOTHED CATS, strong, compact felines—just four or five feet (1.2-1.5 m) long—whose large, muscular jaws and limbs and sharp, seven-inch (17-cm) front fangs made them some of the most powerful hunters of the Ice Age.

SHORT-FACED BEARS, huge, strong predators that were 11 feet (3.3 m) tall—considerably bigger than polar bears today!

MERRIAM'S TERATORNS, stork-like birds that weighed over thirty pounds (11 kg), stood two and half feet (.7 m) tall, and had a wingspan of more than ten feet (3 m)!

WHERE BOGGY MEN AND WOMEN LURK

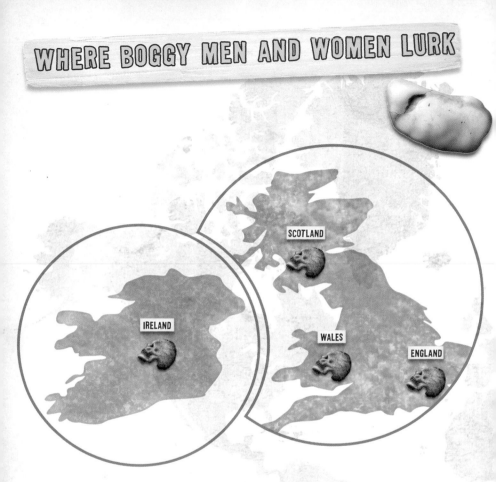

SCOTLAND

IRELAND

WALES

ENGLAND

DID YOU KNOW?

The largest natural asphalt lake—covering about 100 acres (40 hectares) and 250 feet (76 m) deep—is in Trinidad. The giant, smelly tar pit, which legend says was formed as punishment from ancient gods, still bubbles, steams, and sometimes spits fire!

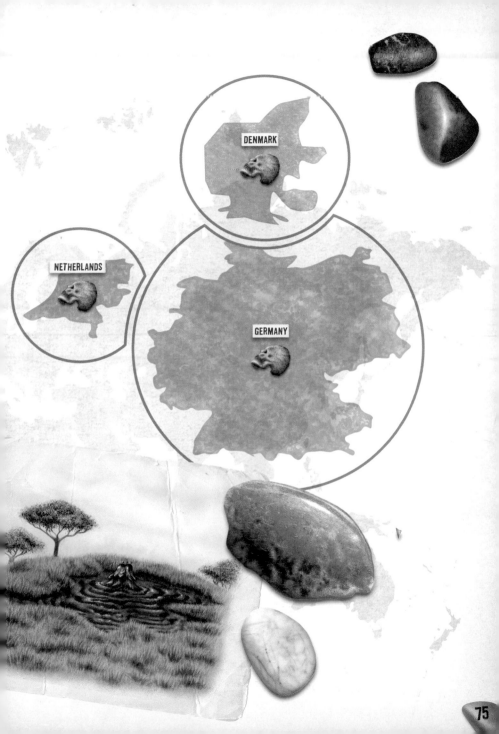

DENMARK

NETHERLANDS

GERMANY

INCREDIBLE
INVESTIGATIONS

After studying the secrets of dino poop, amber, frozen mammals, many kinds of natural mummies, and other remarkable remains, you're ready for some scientific investigations of your own—and some prehistory-inspired fun! Here are a few projects to help you get started.

AND
AMAZING
ACTIVITIES

A T. REX DINO POOP DOORSTOP!

Here's a craft project that will look as impressive as when a Tyrannosaurus produced the real thing millions of years ago!

DINO POOP DOUGH

- 1 cup flour
- 1 cup salt
- 2/3 cup cornstarch
- Small bowl
- 2/3 cup warm water
- Dried rice, pasta, beans, twigs, or anything else you want to add for realistic texture
- Acrylic paint—brownish beige for the most realistic effect!

1. Mix dry ingredients together in the bowl.

2. Add warm water gradually until the mixture can be kneaded into a stiff dough. If the dough is sticky, dust with flour.

3. Now the fun begins! Form your dough into a large, lifelike coprolite. Poke in rice, pasta, beans, twigs, or other items to add texture. (Make sure not to add anything that will melt if you bake the dough.)

4. Once you are finished forming your coprolite, allow it to air-dry for a couple of days before painting. Or, to speed up the process, bake in a slow oven (200°F or 93°C) for 20 minutes or so. (Get an adult to help with using the oven.) Allow to cool.

5. Paint your coprolite creation and allow to dry completely before using. Then watch your guests do a double take when they see what's holding your door open!

IMPRESS YOUR FRIENDS!

EDIBLE AMBER FOR A CROWD

Some amber specimens look pretty enough to eat—and now
you can, with this recipe for a larger-than-life dessert that
rivals the real thing! With a glistening golden base chock full of bugs, frogs,
worms, or whatever else you can imagine, this one-bowl wonder is perfect for
a paleontology-inspired party. Mmm…grab a spoon and dig in!

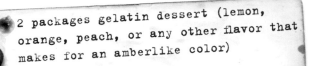

- 2 packages gelatin dessert (lemon, orange, peach, or any other flavor that makes for an amberlike color)

- Glass bowl

- Gummy candy (worms, frogs, flies, spiders…whatever you might like to discover in amber!)

- Licorice whips (optional)

- Cocoa powder (optional)

1. Ask an adult to help you
prepare one package of the
gelatin dessert according to
package directions and pour into
a glass bowl. Refrigerate until set.

2. Poke a nice assortment of candy
bugs and other creatures into the set
gelatin.

3. If you'd like, cut licorice into small pieces and sprinkle on—instant twigs! For "dirt," sprinkle on a tiny amount of cocoa.

4. Ask an adult to help you prepare the second package of gelatin dessert and pour over the top. Refrigerate until set.

FOSSIL CREATIONS

Some fossils form when bones, leaves, and other matter create an imprint on sediment. Over the years, the original matter may disintegrate, but the imprint remains. Create your own decorative fossil mold with this smooth, white dough.

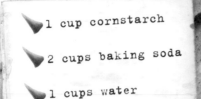

- 1 cup cornstarch
- 2 cups baking soda
- 1 cups water
- Toothpick or pencil

1. Put dry ingredients into a saucepan.

2. With an adult helper, stir in water and cook over medium heat until mixture thickens, about four minutes. (It should look like mashed potatoes.)

3. Remove from heat, and pour onto a plate. Cover with a damp paper towel until it is cool.

4. Knead the dough to make it smooth for shaping. (Store in an airtight container in the refrigerator until ready to use.)

5. Take a Ping-Pong-ball-size piece of dough, and flatten. Choose a fossil design (see below) and copy it onto your dough by carving with a toothpick or pencil.

6. Let the dough air-dry for a day. It will be smooth and rock-like—great to use as a paperweight!

FUN WITH SALT!

CREATE YOUR OWN MUMMY INVESTIGATION!

Who wouldn't want their own mummy! You could go out, find a carcass, and leave it in a bog, cave, or permafrost for thousands of years. Or you could make your very own mummified apple in about a week!

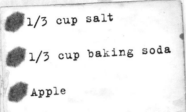

- 1/3 cup salt
- 1/3 cup baking soda
- Apple
- Knife
- 2 plastic cups

1. Mix salt and baking soda together.

2. Ask an adult to help you cut the apple into quarters. Eat two of the quarters. (No, you don't really have to. But you only need two apple quarters for this experiment!)

3. Place each apple quarter in a plastic cup.

4. Carefully pour the salt and baking soda mixture over one of the apples. Make sure to cover it completely.

5. Leave the other apple quarter alone in its cup, with no salt or baking soda. Put your cups out of the way for a week. (Keep them out of direct sunlight.)

6. After a week, check on your apple quarters. Remove the apple in the salt and baking soda mixture and compare it with the other apple quarter. How are they different? (Hint: Ancient Egyptians used salt and soda in their mummifying mixtures!)

GLOSSARY OF TERMS

AMBER: fossilized tree resin that is a hard, translucent substance, usually yellow-orange

ASPHALT: a thick, dark, naturally occurring substance that is a product of decomposing ancient sea creatures; used as glue and for paving and waterproofing

CARBON–14 DATING: a method to determine the age of organic material; also called radiocarbon dating

CARCASS: the partially-decomposed body of a dead animal

CARNIVORE: a meat eater

COPROLITE: fossilized feces

DECAY: to rot

DECOMPOSE: to break down into separate elements

DESICCATE: to dry

DNA: the abbreviation for deoxyribonucleic acid, DNA is a code within cells containing all genetic information of an organism.

FAUNA: animal life in a particular place or period

FLORA: plant life in a particular place or period

FOLIAGE: leaves

FOSSIL: preserved evidence of ancient animals or plants

GASTROLITHS: gizzard stones

HERBIVORE: a plant eater

ICE AGE: period of geologic time when the earth cools and ice covers a significant amount of the planet's surface. When capitalized, Ice Age refers to the most recent period of time when the earth cooled, which started in the Pleistocene epoch.

INCLUSIONS: plants, animals, dirt, and other debris found in fossilized resin

LAGOON: a shallow body of water

MOLT: to shed

PEAT: the remains of bog plants, usually mosses; used as fuel and fertilizer

PERMAFROST: a permanently frozen layer of soil

POLYMERIZATION: the process by which small molecules combine chemically to produce a very large molecule

RESIN: a thick, sticky substance that certain types of trees produce

SAUROPODS: a group of long-necked plant eaters that were the largest of all dinosaurs

SEDIMENT: material that settles to the bottom of a liquid

SPAGNAN: a chemical produced by sphagnum moss that works as a preservative

TERPENES: strong-smelling chemicals that trees and plants produce; responsible for the plants' fragrance

WHERE TO SEE
REMARKABLE REMAINS OF THE PAST

Amazing remains may be as close as your own backyard, park, or school fields! Okay, so maybe you won't discover a frozen woolly mammoth the next time you go for a stroll, but you can see some extraordinary finds at museums throughout North America. Here are some places to start.

FOR DINO POOP AND OTHER PALEONTOLOGY FINDS:

AMERICAN MUSEUM OF NATURAL HISTORY
New York, NY

CARNEGIE MUSEUM OF NATURAL HISTORY
Pittsburgh, PA

CLEVELAND MUSEUM OF NATURAL HISTORY
Cleveland, OH

DALLAS MUSEUM OF NATURAL HISTORY
Dallas, TX

DENVER MUSEUM OF NATURE & SCIENCE
Denver, CO

THE FIELD MUSEUM
Chicago, IL

FLORIDA MUSEUM OF NATURAL HISTORY
Gainesville, FL

NEW MEXICO MUSEUM OF NATURAL HISTORY AND SCIENCE
Albuquerque, NM

ROYAL SASKATCHEWAN MUSEUM
Regina, Saskatchewan
Canada

SMITHSONIAN NATIONAL MUSEUM OF NATURAL HISTORY
Washington, DC

STERNBERG MUSEUM OF NATURAL HISTORY
Hays, KS

UNIVERSITY OF CALIFORNIA, BERKELEY
Museum of Paleontology

FOR AWE-INSPIRING AMBER AND INCLUSIONS:

AMBER RESEARCH LABORATORY, VASSAR COLLEGE
Poughkeepsie, NY

AMERICAN MUSEUM OF NATURAL HISTORY
New York, NY

THE FIELD MUSEUM
Chicago, IL

MUSEUM OF COMPARATIVE ZOOLOGY, HARVARD UNIVERSITY
Cambridge, MA

ROYAL ONTARIO MUSEUM
Toronto, Ontario M5S
Canada

SMITHSONIAN NATIONAL MUSEUM OF NATURAL HISTORY
Washington, DC

UNIVERSITY GALLERY, UNIVERSITY OF DELAWARE
Newark, DE

UNIVERSITY OF CALIFORNIA, BERKELEY
Berkeley, CA

FOR MIGHTY MAMMOTHS AND OTHER ICE AGE ANIMALS:

THE ACADEMY OF NATURAL SCIENCES
Philadelphia, PA

ALASKA MUSEUM OF NATURAL HISTORY
Anchorage, AK

AMHERST COLLEGE MUSEUM OF NATURAL HISTORY
Amherst, MA

CANADIAN MUSEUM OF NATURE
Ottawa, Ontario
Canada

CARNEGIE MUSEUM OF NATURAL HISTORY
Pittsburgh, PA

CLEVELAND MUSEUM OF NATURAL HISTORY
Cleveland, OH

DALLAS MUSEUM OF NATURAL HISTORY
Dallas, TX

DENVER MUSEUM OF NATURE & SCIENCE
Denver, CO

PAGE MUSEUM, LABREA TAR PITS
Los Angeles, CA

SANTA BARBARA MUSEUM OF NATURAL HISTORY
Santa Barbara, CA

SMITHSONIAN NATIONAL MUSEUM OF NATURAL HISTORY
Washington, DC

UNIVERSITY OF MICHIGAN MUSEUM OF PALEONTOLOGY
Ann Arbor, MI

UTAH MUSEUM OF NATURAL HISTORY, UNIVERSITY OF UTAH
Salt Lake City, UT

YALE PEABODY MUSEUM OF NATURAL HISTORY
New Haven, CT

FOR BOG PEOPLE AND OTHER NATURAL MUMMIES:

AMERICAN MUSEUM OF NATURAL HISTORY
New York, NY

ANNISTON MUSEUM OF NATURAL HISTORY
Anniston, AL

THE FIELD MUSEUM
Chicago, IL

SMITHSONIAN NATIONAL MUSEUM OF NATURAL HISTORY
Washington, DC

Excellent traveling exhibits on natural mummies from Europe frequently appear at museums throughout the United States and Canada. Check your local natural history museum for information.

FIELD NOTES

DATE OF DISCOVERY AND A DESCRIPTION OF THE OBJECT:

An archaeologist studies the fossilized remains of living things (including dinosaurs!). Try your hand at archaeology and see what interesting discoveries you can make. Scope out your backyard, a local park, or other safe area, and record your findings on these pages.

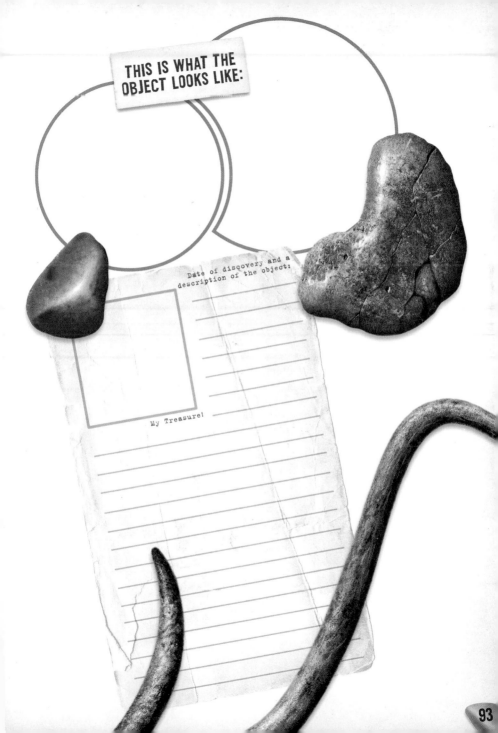

THIS IS WHAT THE
OBJECT LOOKS LIKE:

Date of discovery and a
description of the object:

My Treasure!

DESCRIPTION AND DRAWINGS OF MORE DISCOVERIES I'VE MADE!

DATE OF DISCOVERY:

My Treasure!

FOSSIL LOG

Keep track of the treasures that you find! Be sure to
include the date of your discovery and a description of
the item. You can even draw a picture of what the object
looks like!

(a)
_____
_____
_____
_____
_____
_____
_____

(a)

(b)
_____
_____
_____
_____
_____
_____
_____

(b)

(c)
_____
_____
_____
_____
_____
_____
_____
_____

(c)

(d)
_____
_____
_____
_____
_____
_____
_____

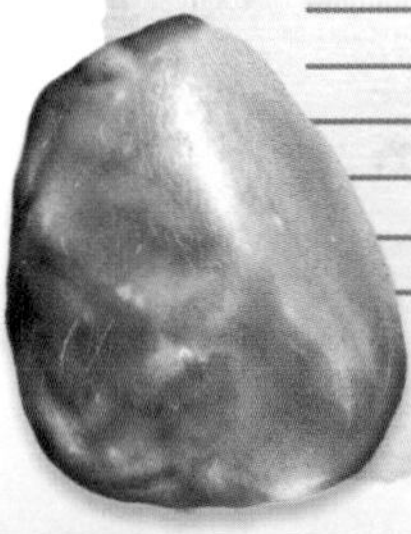

(d)

My Treasure!

HERE'S WHAT I FOUND AND WHEN I FOUND IT!